Phrenology

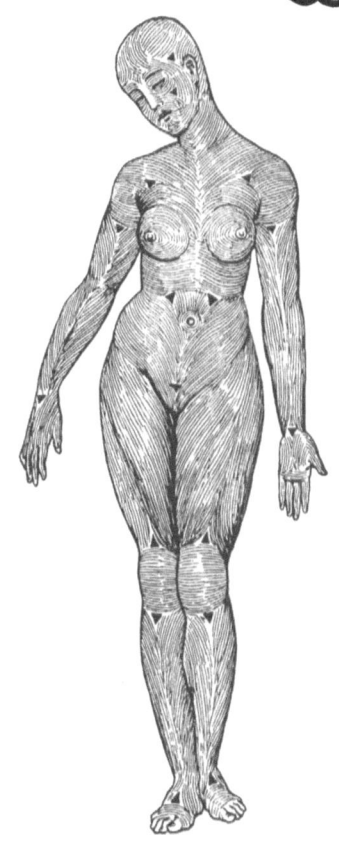

Poems
C.S. Matthews

Columbus, Ohio
empbooks.com

First Edition:10 19 33 34 6 11 1973
ISBN: 979-8-88596-194-3
LOC: 2023942066

Design, Layout, and Edits: Ezhno Martín
Cover: C.S. Matthews
Photos: Products of Shameless Theft

Nothing ever ends poetically. It ends
and we turn it into poetry.
All that blood was never once beautiful.
It was just red.

— Kait Rowkowski

— To all the MMIW2S (Missing and Murdered Indigenous Women, Girls, and Two Spirit) cousins, and the victims and families of residential school violence.

Table of Contents

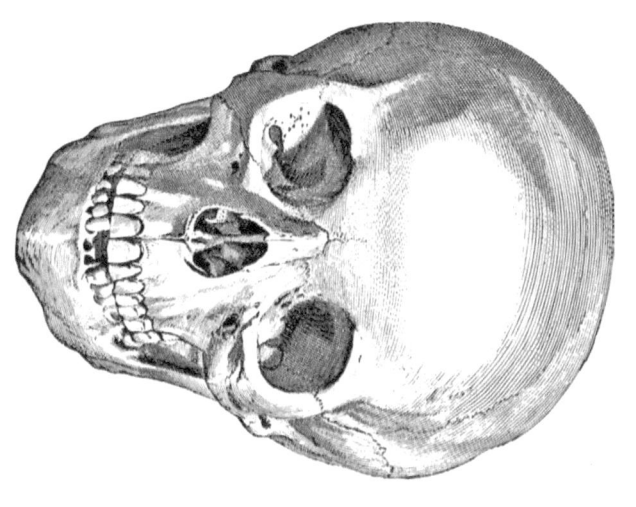

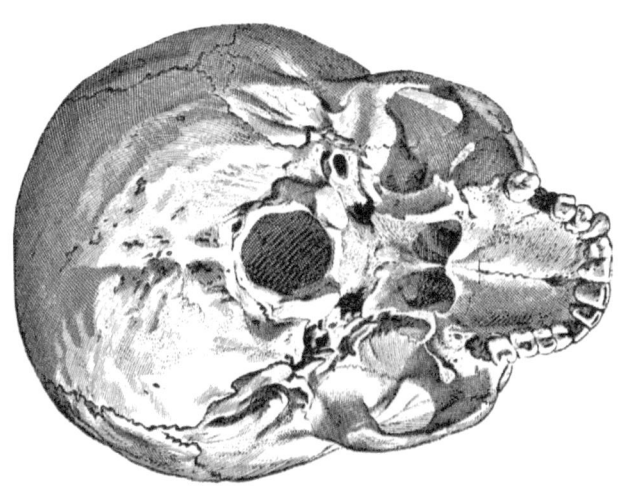

Phrenology

they measure millimeters of bone
to tell us who we are
where we come from

the curve of my incisors
my orbital sockets
hold pools of blue
despite their shape

I am a mixed thing
with an under bite hiding
the gap in my teeth

I broke the extra bone in my foot,
feet whose ancestors were removed
by hands whose decedents counterfeit art
in styles that were stolen

I am a mixed thing
who dreams in a language
I'm learning to speak
from a tongue that was colonized
at birth...

how will you measure me

After Oxygen

I lost my breath in a car wreck
and he stole it with closed vents
- carbon monoxide
- - poisoning the mind

after my brother hung himself
- to get off

after my father choked him
- to move on

and my father stopped breathing
- only after

and my mother stopped hearing
- only after I asked for help

before my asthma went away
- replaced by a hand on my throat
- - a noose on my neck

and I learned the pleasure of suffocating
- trying to end it

maybe my father needed the dopamine
- after my brother died

maybe my brother needed the rush
- after my father choked him

maybe my body learned to love
a lack of oxygen

oxytocin was used to induce me
my father pulled me into the world
by my black right arm
- no blood flow
- - nerve damage

I can't feel a thing
- am I used to the lack of circulation?

when I was five
my father wrote a suicide note
- refused to take me to my mother
said he take me with him

this was after my brother died
after he clogged the vents
- to end us all

before he died

before I was held by my throat
- above a balcony

before I hung myself
-learned how not to breathe...

but after my brother died
after oxygen

Dial Tones

sometimes I call your number
to hear your voice
asking for messages
but your phone has been disconnected
for fourteen years
and I doubt I'd recognize
the sound of you
and I don't know how I'd respond
to hearing it

there's a recording haunting my shelf
of us when I was five
and I'm terrified to play it
hear you speak
see your face move
I think you are just a picture now
but I still call
just to hear dial tones drone

Man

my father once took me aside
he closed his fist around a pinecone
when his fingers uncoiled
the pinecone was unharmed
he handed it to me
and it broke in my palm

he said that

I'd be a man
when I could hold firmly
without harming

maybe it's better that he died
before learning how wrong he was

Teeth

- in dreams
I bite down hard enough
for my teeth to shatter
and I swallow the fragments
- feel their sharp edges
- - cutting my esophagus

- in reality,
my molars slowly chip away
- cut my tongue

fragile from the steroids
they gave me as a child
- to help me breathe

they didn't consider my teeth

neither did he
- upon breaking my incisor

I often find myself considering
- everything
every molecule
- - every aspect of my body
- how it relates

I once read that
we physically hold our trauma

I feel it in my hips

- the way my knees lock

- - when I'm touched

- every sigh of exasperation

- - for every unspoken word

a body is holistic
- even if not whole

the fractures tell a story

if I can only catch my breath
long enough to speak it

Depo

you stole my identity with my tooth
- it was repaired
but the shape was wrong

gone was the gap
- gone the curve

it sticks out in my mouth
- centimeters of bone
and used to catch my lip

I bled there
- in the back seat of your 97 Camry

on the way back from the dentist
- flyers in your window
reading of your great replacement myth

They're Taking Our Jobs

like your daughter took my innocence

I was five and she was ten
- the first time

you spoke of god and divinity
but she raped me repeatedly

two years

and I carry the scars between my legs

divinity

was it divinity that impregnated a Virgin?
did Mary consent?
did my Ancestors?

Divinity

I was made to believe I wasn't whole
- under your god's eye
I was dirty

you knew and did nothing
- I wonder where she learned torture,
- - are there scars between her legs

do they match my own?

soon to be covered in incisions
- rectified by ceremony
- - that inks lines on my cheeks

but for now

a needle culls the ache

Dyclo

pry my tongue from
biting jaws
that render meat pulp

I can't eat meat

my intestines convulse
my throat closes

and my teeth are
shards of glass

I grind them down in sleep

until they are pews
at the pulpit
tongue lashing out
to find purchase

it grips the edges
of their eaves
working holy wrath
on them

until nerves fire
a revelation

and the tongue spits blasphemy
a condemnation

of a creator who builds
broken things
until left begging for relief

- - only to lose my tongue

Scales

I can feel myself
- if I focus

every joint
- ligament
pulling under skin
- arthritis swelling

my intestines slither
- to digest
- - the thought of food

my teeth ache
- at the thought of you

and the weight slips from bone
until I am bones and ache
- joints that swell

but I remember the weight

and forget to eat

Consumption

I used to say that I'd come out
- when I was thin enough

I used to say that I'd come out
- if I wasn't so tall

when I was sixteen
and threw my back out
I didn't realize that I'd stop growing

then, at eighteen
my stomach
cut me down to size

I already had issues
- from time I was fourteen on
but everything I ate hurt
- and I was in constant pain

so I stopped eating
- it hurt anyway
I thought it'd be easier to
- just to go without it
- - not deal with it

I started blacking out
- losing hair

I know it was from a lack of nutrition
- but the nutrition hurt
so I let my stomach shrink

I saw the weight slipping away
and I felt kind of beautiful

I was in constant pain
- feeling sick all the time
and I couldn't even stand upright
- without blacking out

I realized
that I never really talked about this part
- I was ashamed

but I started to love the empty feeling
- started to love the way I looked
when I cinched my waist into a 24
I liked how size zero pants fit me

and I was afraid that if I'd eat
it'd hurt
- but also
- - afraid put the weight back on

and the weight was slipping off so fine
- and I was slimming down
- -like a red vine

so I stopped eating almost all together
- got by drinking protein shakes
- - and that was enough

they prescribed muscle relaxers
-I found out later that muscle relaxers
- - mixed with anti-anxiety meds
- - - feels like an opiate

but in that moment
it was enough
to take a muscle relaxer for the pain
- a shake to keep the darkness at bay
I didn't have an appetite anymore
        —   I think my body forgot
                - - what it was like to eat

so I stopped

just enough to get by
- started measuring everything obsessively
to make sure I got just enough
- not too much

I started working out
because I wanted to be fit
- I know that was some comp-het bullshit
- - but I wanted a six-pack

because my body was thin enough
I could see my abdomen
- do a pull up
- - for the 1st time
and it made me so happy
- even though I was blacking out
- - in constant pain

the muscle relaxers took that edge off
- made me lose focus --- consciousness

I spent my days working in a greenhouse
- 120 degrees
- - nine hours a day
eating just enough to survive

looking back on it
I guess I organically developed an eating disorder
from my bodies disordered eating
but I can't imagine
ever wearing the same pants again

I still have them

they have hair ties
holding the belt loops together
so they'd fit me

I lost 160 pounds and months
from illness
- or malnutrition
from choice
- or decision
I lost the weight

but still fear it will come back again

Stretch Marks and Other Scars

I am at home
beneath skin
stretched over bone
in thin sheets

my back is a web of scars
from the whip that tore
across my skin
as you starved me
in a garage
oat meal in a tin pan

I was too big
you said
before slamming my head
into walls
again and again

so I built walls
disassociated
to forget the way my blood
looked on pavement

how your hand felt around my neck
the sun on my back
as I dig in the desert
without water

but sometimes
I'm back there
starching my uniform at three am
while you burn me...

and finger the scars

Æpathy

I just peeled off my toenail
didn't even notice the pain

can't say I know why I did it
but blood stains mar the door

maybe my SSRI
isn't working

or maybe my mind
has turned to jerky

but my toe is weeping
and my head feels empty

my thoughts are static
 I feel like quitting

might be hormonal
medicine making me whole

might be possession
devil trying to steal my soul...

but who gives a fuck
if I can't even be bothered to care

First Taste of Smoke

he passed me a cigarette
three days or so
after the camera crews filmed volunteers
feeding us in that shelter on the border

he passed me a cigarette
even though I was a twelve y/o asthmatic
who had sworn never to smoke

he passed me a cigarette,
because the gash in my side
was still oozing from the night before

I had been stabbed and was lucky
that it just clipped my hip
but the man saw the war in my eyes
and passed me a Lucky Strike

and we struck up in silence

me pretending to inhale
'cause my side throbbed with every breath
and my head swam

him pretending to not want to ask

we stood there silent
I couldn't even get my thoughts in line
so I just let them slip by

watching beat-to-hell lowriders
bouncing down streets
that no crew had touched

I don't know if it was disassociation
or zen
but I felt empty
like that knife took more than skin

I don't remember thinking it
before hearing my voice say

I guess I've got a pussy now,
and life is fucking me sideways

and we laughed
even though everything hurt

but when the laughter stopped
I couldn't get the echo of those words
to leave me

and I laid awake
listening to the distant pops of guns
and sirens
thinking about it until the sun
rose and flooded the halls
outside our cubical of a room

and I wandered to the bathroom
to change my bandages
before my mom could worry

and ran my finger along the raised edges
where my shit sewing skills pulled
wondering if it hurt this much to get fucked

Immolation

do martyrs feel pleasure
in self-flagellation?

how immersive is immolation?

- the kiss of flames on skin

is it sexual?
- spiritual?

were they abused as children?

taught to love the whip?
- the kiss?

Do my kisses hurt?

Is the rush of adrenaline pleasure?

tortured men feel that rush

- that feeling of falling

it's my favorite sensation

Mom

1.

when I was young
and stuck in the battles of split custody
my mom told me to look to the moon
and she'd be looking too
and we'd be together in that moment

sometimes I'd imagine
I could see her there
face imprinted on lunar light

she used to sing a song
about how everything in existence
longed to be close to me
each night before I'd go to sleep

the last time I heard her sing it
was when I was at my lowest
I don't think she knew
I had just survived my eleventh attempt

even thinking about
how her voice has aged
brings me to tears
and I long to hear that song

2.

through everything I survived
she had to watch me go through

my mom survived too
through years of abuse
and tried her best to shield me
and my siblings

but poverty is a bitch
and she stayed with my dad
for love but also security
what with four kids and a teacher's salary

she found my brothers body
my fathers abuse got worse
he tried to kill us in grief

plugged the vents

that's when she left him
worked three jobs to provide
but three kids became two
when my other brother decided to stay

and two became one
when my sister ran away

3.

she quit teaching to become a server
to provide
worked Wal-Mart at night
and I didn't see her much

until she married the babysitter
and her health went to shit
after his daughter
– who raped me –
poisoned her

but we had a middle-class security
from behind dead bolted bedroom doors
and she saved enough to run again
to some folks she thought were friends

4.

they took everything
while she was bedridden
and I was beaten and starved
forced to recite Proverbs
for a tin pan of oatmeal

she was half deaf and disabled
but dragged herself from bed
to take us once again on the run

but they caught her by the throat
beat me
until we left in police cruisers
to a homeless shelter
they called the abuse *reverse racism*

- haven't trusted a cop since

5.

we had nothing
but the clothes on our back
when we booked a train to St. Louis
grabbed what we could

- left the rest

her dad picked us up
and brought us to a tiny
midwestern town
where her health got worse
and I learned to provide

but her strength and pride
never shrank

Sock

we used to use dryer lint to start fires

the small bits
of discarded fuzz

when I was fourteen
I melted my sock into my foot
with hot grease

had to pick out the pieces

when it got infected
I sterilized an Exact-O Knife
cut out the bad bits
and found
where the fuzz had stuck to bone

//

The first time a knife cut me
I was carving
and it was my dead arm
I didn't even notice
until the wood was wet
red

///

there was no pain when I was stabbed
not at first
just a scraping of metal on bone

the pain came later
during the sleepless nights
in a homeless shelter

I don't think it was the pain
that kept me awake
maybe the fear of them finding us
or the soft pops of gun fire
in the distance

////

I later learned to stop cutting myself
by heating a butter knife on a stove
laying it across my skin
so much cleaner
no messy scars
just ghost lines

||||

when the doctor later examined my foot
he told me I had done well
gave me a salve
and a smile

I had plenty of practice to that point
examining my body with sterilized blades
using them to shape wood
flesh
making my flesh wooden
in my mind
as to distance the sting

there is a dent in my foot
where I rendered my flesh
but I barely notice it
mainly miss the sock

Tomorrow

There is no stronger love
than the embrace of earth
after the rope snaps and
leaves you gasping for tomorrow

Homemade Toys

when I was thirteen
I looked at post-op pictures
- to see if I could tell

I told myself it was so I would know
- if the woman I was with was born that way

but I didn't want to be with anyone
- not that way

and the first time I inserted anything
it was a Dollar Tree hairbrush

I told myself it was to
feel what she would

but I had no interest in being in anyone

porn never turned me on
but I forced myself to watch it

rubbed myself raw
trying to feel something
other than boredom

I taught myself to go down
by watching how-to's on YouTube
- 'cause I wanted my partner to cum

and I liked that

liked the feeling of being filled
- got off to erotica
- - with homemade toys

I thought maybe I was gay
but boys disgusted me,
and women are beautiful
- funny how I would learn I was right
- - but in the wrong body

When I was fifteen
I told a friend that I was Asexual
that the thought of being with someone felt wrong
- like the bits between my legs belonged to
someone else
- - and I was just holding them

When I was sixteen
I told a lesbian that I thought I was trans
she told me she was gay
and asked why I told her

I guess its because I felt safer
with queer women

Coming Out

the first time I wore my regalia in public
was at a protest we organized
Indigenous Day of Rage Against
Colonialism and Capitalism

we marched under a flag I designed
Fist with Feather
Red and Black
Anarcho-Indigenous Rage

The next time
we didn't march
just lit 7,370 candles
one for each dead body found
to that point

the first time
I screamed and sang the AIM song
lighting a fire on the river walk
and nearly collapsed in the heat
when it was over

the second time
I silently wept
trying to keep the candles lit

I came out
that first time
embraced my ancestors
and myself as queer

the second time
I was considering de-transition
out of exhaustion
from too many sexual assaults
and advances

44

I began a painting
when the bodies were found
did ceremony
held vigils

but I often dream of my own body
hair cut
tongue split
raped and half buried
in a field

No Thanks

whiskey glass passing
in incendiary apathy
masking colonial tidings of
good will from the gates of hell

as your transphobic family
says grace to a god that damned you
and all of your ancestors

while empty traditions
of yuletide fictions
make the friction in your familial spaces
stand as erect as a rapist prick
at any glance of your skin

because

strategically hidden scars
hide war time realities
and predators tip prey better
than fighters

and you fight to bite back the urge
to say just that

as your MAGA-hippie-aunt
misgenders you while talking about
her Rekei practice

over instant potatoes
a plant
whose growth fed your ancestors
reduced to powder

as white as your moms side

as white as their fragility
knowing you're mixed

as white as the hate
your father faced

and you'e the ingrate
for giving thanks
on any day but this

Indian Burial Grounds

cupboards shudder
rafters quake
doors slam
as a priest screams
in broken Latin
about some dude with a beard

then silence

the angry Indian spirits are gone
god save the queen
(or at least her corpse)
halle-fuckin-lujah

that's how it always goes
on the screen
Good and Evil
facing off
and we're always evil
the church always wins

nobody talks about how
if our burial grounds were haunted
every rectory would be overrun
by dead children

how most cities
would have small pox symptoms

no one realizes
that every military base
would be ravaged
by poltergeist warriors
that farms would be as barren
as the bones they tilled over

they don't talk about
how missionaries would be chased
by one legged Indians
or how nuns would be followed
by masses of burned babies

the only real thing monsters
are haunted by is the living
and those who refused to die

Lesbihonest

I had a crush on her then
just like I had a crush
on so many other queer women
not out of lust
and the crush wasn't really on them
but on a desire to be fem

and there is that old joke
about gay women
and not knowing
if you wanted to be her
or with her

I think every crush I had
was an homage

I should have known
when it was always book characters
their internal world is what I desired
until Ruby Rose

they struck such a chord
in pitch perfect three
I knew in that moment that it was both

because I actually wanted someone
for the first time

but not in a masculine way

I want them to take me
to taste them

I realized then
that my gender anxiety went deeper
and I definitely wasn't straight
because I'm not cis

I tried playing along socially
but it was an act

I tried playing along sexually
and I'm still rectifying the trauma

but when I found myself
I found comfort in my sexuality

I guess the first person I came out to
- that lesbian from my high school
I came out to her because I'm a lesbian too
it just took a few extra steps
for me to realize it

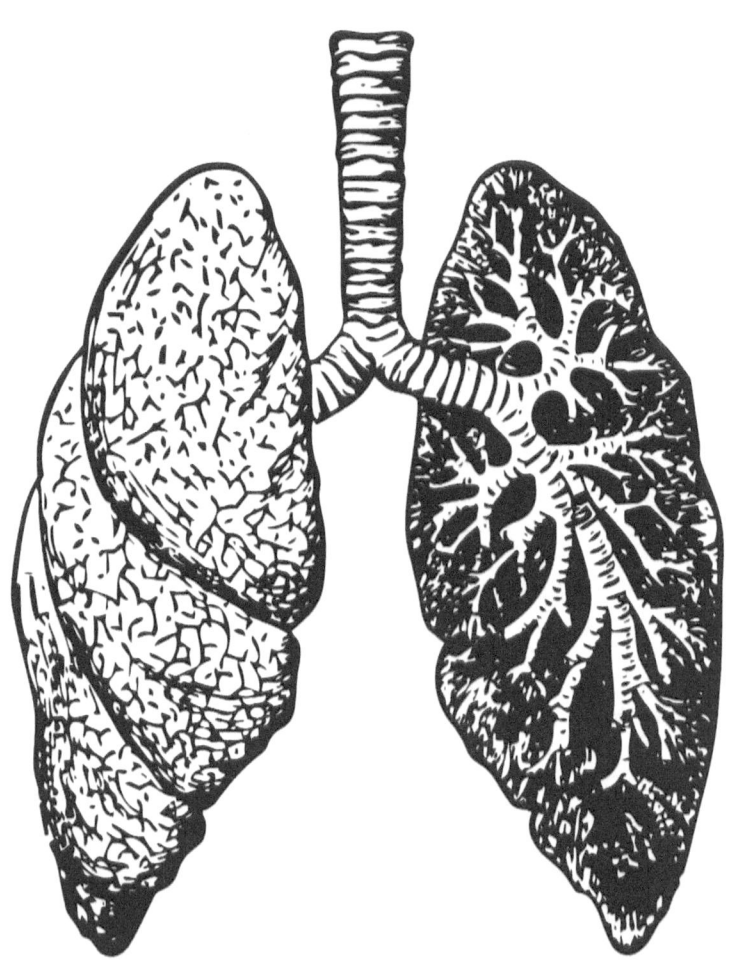

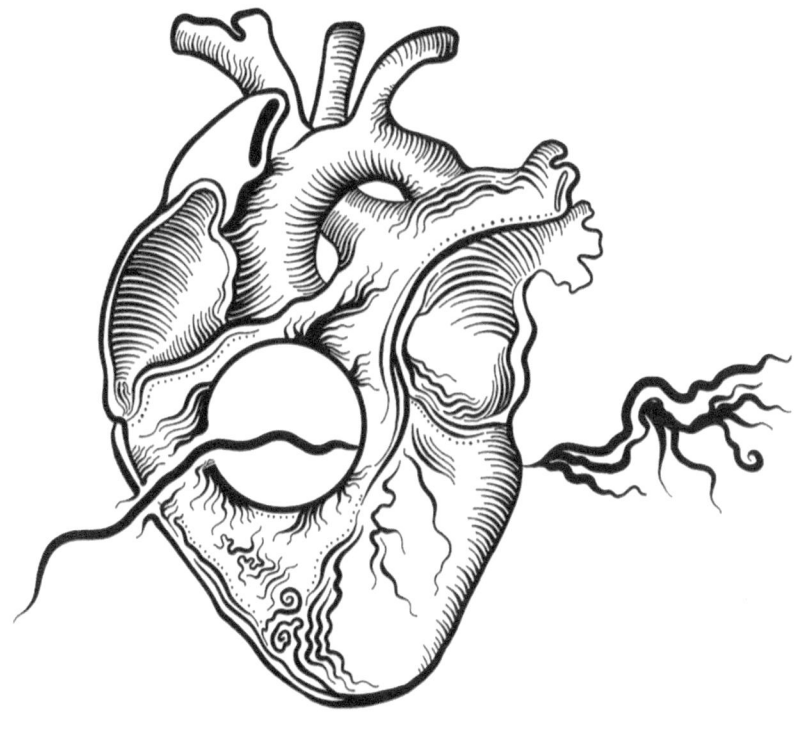

Billiards

did you know she was a terf
the first time she fucked you?
did the subtleties of language
queue you in for a pocket
before she lined your cue
up for a bank shot...

before she missed consent
and you lost time

how didn't you make the connection
when she called surgery mutilation?
why did you go back for game after game
when she essentialized you to the bits ;
the tool she could use to get off
as you try not to disassociate again

but you didn't feel it then
or for a long time after

how didn't you know it was rape
when everything collapsed in the after?
When you called every subsequent encounter
Exposure Therapy
and the first time was the catalyst
that made you seek the surgery
you always wanted

and the cueball always slides in
behind the 8 when money is on the line

so, you tried to tap it in

by talking it out with your partner
friends;
bank it off that right clip
make it something less incendiary...

but the cue always slips
and sends the ball sideways

into panic field thoughts
of seeing her again
despite the fact that she
probably didn't mean harm
but you know it was rape

as much as you denied it
try to hold on to your agency in post

you can't unfuck a bankshot
once the ball is rolling
can't undo or uncue it...
you just watch the white slip into
your opponent's grasp

and know they control the green

Golden

not everything gay is golden
I have been raped by queer women
-as a child and an adult

I have been groped by
hands reaching out of the closet
-grasping for authenticity

I have been devoured by
10,000 hungry eyes
-shelled things waiting to hatch

all they see are my feathers,
me as some exotic bird
-to cage or feast upon

so, they grip me until
my bones shatter
-because they forget

 --what it takes to fly

Make Me a Costume

I feel like that
consignment store headdress
I found when I went home

it was the first time in nine years
since the fire
and the forest of my youth
had been replaced by
so many condos

the shop owner told me
that a Crow man brought the headdress in
- it was his grandfathers
because he couldn't pay the bills

two lanes of the highway
are train tracks now
and the hospital my father died in
is a rec center

the feathers of that war bonnet
were bent and broken
and the bead work was coming undone
from cracking leather

It took me three tries
to find my brothers grave
everything was so different
and the balloon popped in transit

I can imagine my old home as a caldera
after the super volcano goes off
and I imagine myself
a broken war bonnet
in the ashes

Pass Over

maybe there is blood on my doorway
stepping in though entry
in a bar lit by halogen
set in a town
whose population is
less than my graduating class

there's an odd observation
that in this moment
I'm passing
- no second glances
- - save for my assets

just a gnawing in my stomach
- at the thought and
- - I'm realizing
that this keeps happening

'cause the thought of passing disgusts me
- the cops that hit my cousins
- - hit on me

yet in a red state,
there is safety
in stealth modeing
my way past drunk men

- but what if they notice
- - the size of my hands

- - -how tall I am

will the beating be protected
by claims of trans-panic?

what if I look too pretty
            —   *will they assault me*

        - - like so many before?

too nervous to be less than sober
but it seems god has passed over
- a sacrifice of sanity
and maybe I can escape
the prison of passage
in the baring straights

- at least for me
but how many are left bleeding
- dead and raped
- - shot by police
for not having the privilege of passing?

But is it really privilege?
-      the need to hide for safety

why is our goal to disappear
when so many are never seen
- save for porn
- - crime
- - - and comedy

so why the fuck do I feel relief
- at the thought of being unseen
when that might just be
the thing that fucking ends me

but here I sit in a bar
- sipping on a glass of gin
as Pharoah mourns his son

and I'm wondering if he was trans

Real

shit
I'm overthinking again
like what she meant when she asked
if my partner was a *real woman*

damn
now I'm thinking about language
and if I'm a *real Indian*
if I learn 'Nish secondhand

Is there a word for *real* in Anishinaabemowin?

am I a Zhaagananosh for not knowing it?

less real for being born with a dick?

the worst bit is knowing
what she meant
when she said it
or that she didn't have intent
but
- devils
- - road
- - - pavement
- - - - fuck it
I'm real tired of good intent
making people feel
that they have the right
to be invasive

That Edgy Self-Loathing Poem

I'm an animated corpse
of contrivances
a hodge-podge
sampling of serendipitous
serenity on a scalpel lined stick

you could call me beautiful
if you were morbid enough
for my gangrenous skin
to entice

Vlad would wince
at the state of me
before masturbating fervently

there are online challenges
to see who can get off
to pics of me

I'm the zombified queen
of your absolute worst dreams

but you still dream of me
and hide the sock
from your wife

Orthostatic Hypotension

sometimes I stand too quickly
with the sole purpose of
seeing divinity
in the white-black lines
that interstate wind
across my vision

until I'm blind

falling for safe havens in
west station
trains leading anywhere but
here
where i stand in approximation

of human

still too much a man
to be perceived as divine
Femininity leaking like an open wound-
I have no womb
so, I rise to fall,

seeking absolution

from the sins of my birth
being wrong
Taking too long to form
the mass of me

center well of gravity

and I'm falling blind

to feel something more than shame

Wendigo

as far as i can tell,
stories of the Wendigo
start with the colonizers arriving

the spirit of greed
consuming
until families consume themselves

I was told they ran through the treetops

*my brothers tree was topped
the one over his grave*

some stories treat them like vampires
rising from the dead

the hunters told stories of a man
butchering his family

*my father tried to kill us
after my brother died*

out of an insatiable hunger

he ate them

*my father threw the meat scale at my mother
when the doctor said to cut back*

and colonization infects our communities
as we chant
Land Back
in the colonizers tongue
praying to their god

"

*my father learned to pray
when he married my mom*

and the Wendigo spirit possessed hunters
who were paid to hunt their own
taught to scalp by Hamburg invaders

*my hair looks like my mother's
curls part Irish
part Creole from my father*

and we banded together under AIM
to fight back
became complacent on table scraps

*my mother's ancestor hunted
my Creole family
during the civil war
tortured and lynched them
cut babies from the living bellies
of my Seminole relatives*

but the war has never ended,
despite them taking our children in the night
cutting their hair and tongues
throwing them in mass graves

*my family tree is a Wendigo
my body the collected parts of rape
genocide
its roots are consumption
cannibalistic
killing itself to feast
grow*

so we fight in Standing Rock
in the streets of Oakland
we scream our stolen languages at the pope
from stolen tongues
we burn churches
and plant our Three Sisters in their wake

we are the survivors of genocide that runs circles
as Wendigos wear our feathers

*I wept when they found the graves
wanted to scream
but there was no air
I wanted to burn
but I couldn't stand
spoke to a survivor at two am
talked her off her roof
convinced her to go to ceremony
she drove 200 miles that night*

our siblings our stolen
in red
highway of tears
a trail of tears
on stolen land
littered with stolen bodies
our bodies
consumed
as our medicine is misused
to get a buzz
a high
and addiction steals our lives

*we lit over 7000 candles
they've found over 10000 bodies
eleven schools out of 500
when the pope came
I folded like a prayer tie
my hair is heavy on my head*

Paint The Sky In Watercolor
(PTSD)

you are holding me
as the sky erupts around us
and I am back there mopping the floor
homeless
he is stumbling in the doorway
a hole in his side
bleeding on the linoleum
and it is almost like watercolor
as sky is awash in color
bombs erupting
and he is bleeding
and it looks like watercolor
and I might be an artist
and I feel the knife in my back
does not hurt
just scrapes bone
and I am bleeding on the pavement
and it looks like oil
and you are holding me
and the sky is erupting
and I am shaking
bombs above us
and he is bleeding
it looks like watercolor on wet linoleum
and I might be an artist
but I do not like watercolor
it scares me
because he is bleeding
and I see my own blood on the pavement

bright and red
as he is bleeding
I have been whipped
I have been stabbed
he has been shot
and I hear it
the guns on the border are blazing
and the sky is flooded by light
and it is bright
you are holding me
and I do not know where I am
and we are walking
but now we are home
and he is bleeding
and the sky is erupting
there are fires everywhere
and they are shining down on us
like stars falling
and his blood is falling
and it looks like watercolor
and I might be an artist
and I feel the knife on my back
as it scrapes bone
and I hear it
guns on the border
and I know it is red
and bright
and it is bleeding
and it is oil
and it is bleeding
and it is oil
and it is watercolor
and the sky is awash in watercolor
and they are falling upon us
drops of stardust
and I feel the knife in my back

and it is loud
and it is bleeding
and there are guns on the border
and he is bleeding
and I am bleeding and we are bleeding
and I do not know where I am
but you are holding me
and I am shaking
and you are holding me
and he is bleeding
and I am bleeding
and the border is a rupture of fire lights
and it looks like watercolor

I might be an artist

Every White Boy

Every White Boy
will tell you about their ego death
while sipping five-dollar whiskey
from a nightmare before christmas coffee mug

they've usually got a tattoo of the hatchet man
if they are over 27
from back before their ego death
they don't regret it
just who they used to be

but they still love Faygo

Every White Boy
starts to question gender
a little to late
and it shows in how they lecture
dominating every conversation
as they drunkenly trauma dump
at two am

and you stay
because you don't want them
to go through it alone

like you did

and they share how they aren't white
or a boy
so you try to help them understand
just what that means

as they talk over you

but you still do that too
from time to time
it's a hard habit to break
feeling like what you have to say
could change the world

sometimes you feel like your words hold weight
and who can blame you
when everyone treated them that way
at least they used to

so you give him the space to fill

he'll take it anyway
they all do now
and they'll understand that soon
so you nod along
while making a graph
a visual aid always helps keep the dysphoria at bay

and you're definitely feeling it
each question more invasive then the last
his conjured understanding
eclipsing your lived experience

but it's a start

Decindian

I learn my culture through stories
my language too
all second-hand passings
does that make me a Decindian?

that the little bits my father passed on
before he passed on
feel like films now

that I have little connection
to my own tribes
and my elders are borrowed

sometimes I feel like
a trading post refugee
and my ancestors have no faces to me

just names
they were stolen
stories caught in the webs
of the Dream Catcher
my father made me

my Mocs have no flaps
because I cant bead

my wedding dress
is a pile of fabric
waiting to be sewn

but no aunties
have taught me the stitches

raised off Rez' to a dying father
who loved John Wayne
as much as his own people

a father whose father left him
in the womb

my skin is my mother's white
but I scar like my father

maybe the scars of absence
are my true heritage

the untied ends
the burrowed stories
I weave them
seeing as I can't sew

John Wayne

my father was a *John Wayne Indian*
he learned his culture from westerns
the Boy Scouts
and Powwows

he was a 50's baby
born of a runaway father
and a alcoholic mother
living from poverty to poverty
in a time of plenty

his dark complexion on curly hair
made him an Indiana oddity
so he learned to weave stories
in the same way he learned
to make Dream Catchers

out of the few traditions he passed down
the Dream Catcher we made together sticks out

I don't know where he learned it
but I learned to wrap feathers
from dissecting his
and my first and last Mocs he made
were Plains Style

I remember sitting on his knee
watching Lord of the Rings and drawing
maybe my art is inherent
like spider webs

Asabikeshiinh made the first Dream Catcher
out of gratitude for being left to live
and in its webs are the stories of my
waking nightmares
- my flashbacks

my father gifted me a tradition
probably learned from a film
from a people who would later take me in
as a trading post refugee

maybe I am a Decindian
and maybe that's okay

Sexton

sometimes I look at trans porn
not because I get off to it
but because seeing bodies
that look like mine
makes me feel kind of beautiful

even if the porn is from a male gaze
the bodies aren't
and beautiful trans girls give me hope
that maybe I'm beautiful

then I think about how depressing it is
to only see yourself in porn
with titles like
Tranny Slut   *Shemale*   *Trapp*

especially when
every unsolicited picture
comes with the same tag-line

I wish there were more stories like mine
more bodies like mine
that people saw more folks like me
so I wasn't so eroticized

I'm tired of feeling like
a colorful bird in a cage
with everyone wanting to pluck a feather

Just an Indian Thing

when my father died
no one had to tell me
I just knew
and there was no sadness
just the quiet of my bed above me
as I curled beneath

I saw him in the small oddities
after

I saw him in the lost Snowy Owl
outside my window
every morning at dawn

I heard him in the wind
coming down from the mountains

maybe it's a Native thing
seeing the dead
in the way the aspen
turn to fire with fall

the way a spider web arches
branches into Dream Catchers

I'd stare at the Dream Catcher
we made together
before bed and think
of the moon full of spiders

and how their webs hold stories

spiders are born knowing how to weave

and I think myself a spider
in how my hands knew the knots of wood
when I found his tools

he was a wood worker
and I learned to play the flute
on his unfinished bodies
using chunks of hard leather to bend air back

I heard him there too
but his voice is lost to me
just the trill of open notes
the sound of owls in the night

his face is in the aspen fire

Self-Love

self-love
is what I call my vibrator at 2am

until the battery dies

and I'm left scrambling for the cord
wanting to finish
so close to the edge

wanting to ride it
run it

knowing the charge will take too long

fuck it

literally
unplug it
run it

but the moment is passing
and the sound is too wet
though I'm drying out

ache in my stomach
the reminder of ecstasy
left unsatisfied

panting
empty
I roll over

tightening my muscles
around the shaft
too dejected to take it out

and I remember that time
my partner called herself
circumstantially sexual

and I never related to anything more

demisexual with a dead battery
stuck halfway in

overthinking what it even means
to be circumstantial
in sexuality

when my drive is as dead
as the battery in my vibrator

Water

sometimes
when you hold water long enough
you forget it is part of you
until it rips itself from you
leaving you a deserted thing

and desertification
leaves scared land
where water once dwelled

I was taught that water is sentient
alive as the land it deserts
in favor of the sky
always to return
if not stolen

water is my polyamorous cousin
it has traveled through all things
until horded by man who thinks to own it
trapped in plastic that then pollutes it

is it irony or the lead that kills us
as we kill our cousin?

Shower

when I was young
an elder told me to give my pain to the water

I'd imagine the pain at the roots of my hair
and I'd let the water carry it
take it away

and every shower became a ceremony
a sacred space
- I open to only you

as I wash pain out of your scalp
run my fingers through your hair
I see prayers written in the silver
and I carry them across your skin
writing in a language without script

and you care for my hair
that sacred record of my life
tracing the lines with a finger
that finds indexes where prayers once sat

and I pray to your skin
as water runs between lips brushing
I write to you in a language lost
- stolen
words that echo in a forgotten space
as you run hands over the scars
parting memories
lessons learned in pain

I want you to hold my stories in your hands
and I want to carry yours

there is medicine in the steam
a subtle smokiness in your breath as we kiss
and the music makes your skin rise
in spite of the heat

I whisper in your ear
as you bite mine

this moment sits infinite in my mind

Sweat Lodge

you don't know what to wear
when you meet your grandfathers
the blankets drive away the light
- weighted by hide
but you know he'll see you
- glowing red
and you know you'll lay your face to the ground
- gasp for air
wheeze prayers out from the stone
- burning
behind the buds on your chest

they burn

a reminder of your years of denial
- of hiding
and he knows you
- chose you for the fire
loves you
- for you are sacred

and afraid

you don't want to disrespect him

he was molded under pressure,
- rolled and washed over
for thousands of years
- to find you
- to honor you
- to love you

to be put through fire
- mined from the ashes
- - dowsed in water
so the steam can carry your prayers

and you want to honor him

- his journey
- - his love
as he honors yours

there have always been owls
they sit in the field where light flickers
- and the light is yellow
faintly
outlining the bones of a harvest

it hides mountains
- their memory a haze
the smoke of fires in your eye
bringing tears as you stare at grandfather
- glowing red
he called to you

you felt it

in the shape of his curves
the chill in your arms as you held him
the pink flecks
- red now

he called
and you answered

you all did

four grandfathers apiece

eighteen stones
- it's a pretty number
right now
as you stare

eighteen

your mouth feels the syllables
the memory of them
- round
- - specked pink
rolling through a river in the mountains
hidden just beyond the smoke
- past the bones
- - the soft yellow light
the sound of the wind in the rafters as you sleep
- dream
- - of the owl in the field
watching

- warning

you glance to him
- in the flames
just through the flap as you circle the pit
- into shadows
whisper silent thanks as the grandfathers
are brought in

the air taste of bear-root

you can barely breathe through the songs
- but sing
feel the grass between your toes
- cold
and you pray

tears mixing with sweat
- dripping from your nose
as you lean forward
- shaking
your words flowing
prayer and song mixing
- flowing
as in your mind you see her

just beyond the smoke
- past the bones
hidden by the light
- no more
the mountains rise
growing from blue seeds planted
- budding
from your chest
- they break free
- - no longer hiding

they rise

and you with them

Che Meegwetch

C.S.Mathews is the author of **Redactable** from *The Grindstone*, co-author of **Fearful Architecture**, as well as the upcoming books **Ecstatic Birth** from *Laughing Ronin Press*, and **Eucharist** from *Pure Sleaze*. Her work can also be found in several journals and anthologies. She is the coeditor of *The Grindstone*, co-host of *Poetry Speaks* and the artist for many a book cover.

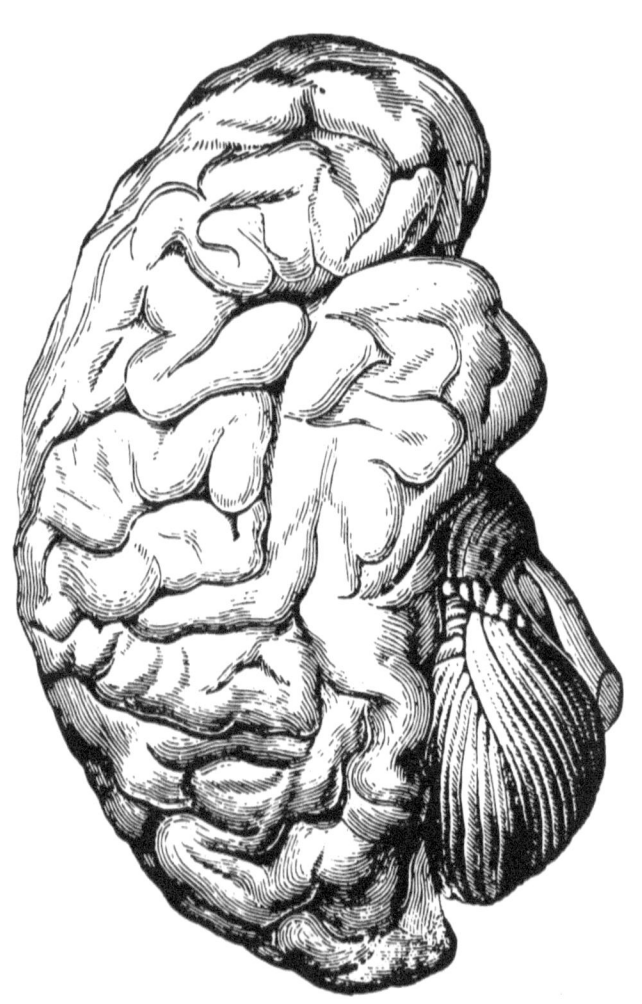